How to Hustle the Urban Dollar

Urban Dollar

The Beginner's How-To Guide

By Christopher Lawson

AuthorHouse™
1663 Liberty Drive
Bloomington, IN 47403
www.authorhouse.com
Phone: 1 (800) 839-8640

Published by AuthorHouse 02/19/2019

ISBN: 978-1-5462-6907-6 (sc)
ISBN: 978-1-5462-6908-3 (hc)
ISBN: 978-1-5462-6906-9 (e)

Library of Congress Control Number: 2019900892

Print information available on the last page.

Any people depicted in stock imagery provided by Getty Images are models,
and such images are being used for illustrative purposes only.
Certain stock imagery © Getty Images.

This book is printed on acid-free paper.

Because of the dynamic nature of the Internet, any web addresses or links contained in this book may have changed
since publication and may no longer be valid. The views expressed in this work are solely those of the author and do not
necessarily reflect the views of the publisher, and the publisher hereby disclaims any responsibility for them.

CONTENTS

INTRODUCTION

Thousands and thousands of books are published yearly in America. Only a small percentage of the books that are published are coming from and speaking to the African American perspective. An even smaller percentage are dedicated to financially educating the urban community. There is a distinct difference between the financial challenges of rural, urban, and suburban communities.

This book is intended to inform the reader on the most basic of levels about financial literacy. Oftentimes in life, we blame the material for being outdated but not the presenter. My goal is to connect the financial world and the inner city by giving guides and examples. Hopefully reading this type of book will spark something and allow those creative juices that you have upstairs to start flowing. Finances are like tools. Each job requires a different one, with a few exceptions that allow one tool to fix multiple projects. Some financial information could be considered the multipurpose tool, but that analogy does not apply to all. Taking the same path that a baby boomer took to gain financial independence probably wouldn't work for millennials. The truth is that times are different now, and the financial path taken in 1980 may not be beneficial to you in 2018.

I believe that stories should be told in their entirety, the good, the bad, and the truth. Then and only then can you make an informed decision. When reading books, I always ask myself, "Am I who the author is thinking of, and is this information applicable to my situation?" This book may be outside of the norm for conservative financial readers, and that's okay because I am not looking for them. I am looking for everyone but them to receive these financial fundamentals with an urban twist. Good luck on the first step of your new journey to financial freedom and enlightenment.

CHAPTER 1

Increasing the Income

Make more money! Now I do not want to mislead any of my readers by making this seem like it is the easiest thing in the world to do, but it is not the hardest thing either. The person who coined the phrase "every penny counts" was probably a hardworking, middle-class individual who likely meant that phrase literally. I am probably stating the obvious here, but what may at first glance seem obvious is oftentimes overlooked.

An additional job is one way of increasing your income, but it is not the only way. Investing your dollars so that they may work for you is another way, which we will discuss in more detail in chapter 4. Much like anything in life, increasing your income has just as much to do with your physical abilities as your mental ones. In some careers, you may have to do more physical work. Other careers may require you to visualize the results, which demands more mental application. People have always said that education is the key. The key to what you ask? I have no idea, maybe it's the key to everything, or maybe it's the key to nothing at all. Either way education is an essential part of the maturation process. The world we live in is constantly evolving, and with the emergence of the internet we have become more connected than ever. Unfortunately, in a job market this does not benefit you. Employers have the upper hand, whether you're talking about salary, retention, or accession. What does this mean? It simply means that companies can pay you less and fire you more quickly because you can easily be replaced in an employers' market. Be open to exploring all your options. Listed below for your reference are charts that show you the change in each individual state's median income.

Median Household Income: Winners and Losers Since 2000							
States & DC	2000 Rank	2015 Rank	Change	States & DC	2000 Rank	2015 Rank	Change
District of Columbia	26	5	21	New Jersey	6	7	-1
North Dakota	42	25	17	Utah	10	11	-1
Wyoming	32	15	17	Arizona	31	33	-2
Iowa	28	16	12	Maryland	1	3	-2
Vermont	33	21	12	New Mexico	44	46	-2
South Dakota	40	29	11	North Carolina	36	38	-2
Washington	20	9	11	Kansas	27	30	-3
Montana	47	37	10	Virginia	11	14	-3
Texas	35	26	9	Alabama	43	47	-4
Nebraska	25	18	7	Minnesota	2	6	-4
New York	30	23	7	Illinois	14	19	-5
Massachusetts	13	8	5	Missouri	17	22	-5
Oklahoma	48	43	5	Rhode Island	22	27	-5
Connecticut	8	4	4	Indiana	29	35	-6
Louisiana	49	45	4	Mississippi	45	51	-6
New Hampshire	5	1	4	South Carolina	38	44	-6
Oregon	21	17	4	Florida	34	41	-7
Tennessee	46	42	4	Hawaii	4	12	-8
Pennsylvania	23	20	3	Kentucky	41	50	-9
West Virginia	51	48	3	Wisconsin	18	28	-10
Alaska	3	2	1	Ohio	19	32	-13
Arkansas	50	49	1	Georgia	24	39	-15
Idaho	37	36	1	Michigan	16	31	-15
California	12	13	-1	Delaware	7	24	-17
Colorado	9	10	-1	Nevada	15	34	-19
Maine	39	40	-1				

Source: Census Bureau, Current Population Survey

Don't be afraid to explore opportunities. One mistake we often make is that after developing a rapport with people or a company, we feel obligated to that organization. The truth is that moving is always an option. With that being said, always be open to exploring every option available. Everything under the sun has a life cycle consisting of an incline, a plateau, and a decline. This is why so many young adults move away from those small towns that they were raised in. The local job market usually has matured and is not able to support the current population. Before moving to a new city, there are obviously things to consider, such as salary, benefits, and the housing market, as well as company incentives. You need to keep in mind that companies are looking for the next best thing, and so should you.

Job loyalty will surely die with the baby boomers. A 401(k) or Roth IRA will increase no matter where you are working as long as you are faithfully contributing to it. While we're on the topic, let's dig into different incentives that may be available. The incentives that come with a job can be just as important as the salary. As the old folks used to say, "There's more than one way to skin a cat." Well, in this case, one plus one is not the only way to get two. While semi unorthodox, two minus zero can also give you two.

Median Household Incomes: Top to Bottom							
States & DC	2015 Median Income	Year of Peak Income	Decline	States & DC	2015 Median Income	Year of Peak Income	Decline
New Hampshire	75,675	2007	-2.0%	Texas	56,473	2015	0.0%
Alaska	75,112	1996	-5.4%	Rhode Island	55,701	2006	-11.8%
Maryland	73,594	2014	-3.5%	Wisconsin	55,425	1999	-14.7%
Connecticut	72,889	1989	-6.7	South Dakota	55,065	2008	-3.1%
District of Columbia	70,071	2015	0.0%	Kansas	54,865	2003	-3.7%
Minnesota	68,730	2000	-7.9%	Michigan	54,203	1999	-17.4%
New Jersey	68,357	2006	-14.6%	Ohio	53,301	2000	-9.9%
Massachusetts	67,861	2001	-3.0%	Arizona	55,248	2001	-8.6%
Washington	67,243	1998	-2.4%	Nevada	52,008	2000	-17.4%
Colorado	66,596	2007	-4.7%	Indiana	51,983	1999	-10.5%
Utah	66,258	2008	-3.8%	Idaho	51,624	2007	-8.2%
Hawaii	61,514	2007	-11.8%	Montana	51,395	2015	0.0%
California	63,636	2006	-2.1%	North Carolina	50,797	1996	-5.2%
Virginia	61,486	2003	-12.9%	Georgia	50,768	2006	-12.5%
Wyoming	60,925	2013	-11.2%	Maine	50,756	2013	-9.2%
Iowa	60,834	2013	-0.6%	Florida	48,825	2006	-9.1%
Oregon	60,834	2015	0.0%	Tennessee	47,330	1999	-8.9%
Nebraska	60,474	2015	0.0%	Oklahoma	47,077	2011	-7.8%
Illinois	60,413	1999	-8.4%	South Carolina	46,360	1996	-11.1%
Pennsylvania	60,389	2015	0.0%	Louisiana	45,922	2009	-8.5%
Vermont	59,494	2013	-10.8%	New Mexico	45,119	2007	-11.0%
Missouri	59,196	2000	-4.6%	Alabama	44,509	1998	-15.5%
New York	58,005	1989	-0.2%	West Virginia	42,824	2007	-11.0%
Delaware	57,756	2014	-16.7%	Arkansas	42,798	2007	-8.2%
North Dakota	57,415	2014	-5.6%	Kentucky	42,387	1998	-19.5%
United States	56,516	1999	-2.4%	Mississippi	40,037	2000	-15.2%

Note: Peak year = highest real median income: source: U.S. Census Bureau. Current Population Survey

Money must be viewed beyond its surface. The dollar is merely a tool or a key that you are using to get you into the desired places or situations that you seek. The more opportunities an individual has, the greater the chances of that person reaching his or her goals. Personally, I reject the negative stereotype that surrounds moving backward. Sometimes moving backward is essential before moving forward.

Find a job that offers incentives, per diem, mileage, travel, and allowances. These sorts of incentives can greatly increase your income, depending on your profession and how frequently you can use such incentives. While the phrase "C.R.E.A.M." (Cash Rules Everything Around Me) still stands true even since its creation the Wu-Tang Clan created it back in 1993, understanding how these incentives work can really boost your income level.

- **Pros of Increasing Your Income:** *open-mindedness, more opportunities, less financial stress*
  Remember that increasing your income is not just about adding more dollars to the equation. If you can find creative ways to solve some of your financial problems, then you can increase your income without changing your salary.

- **Cons of Increasing Your Income:** *greed, higher consumption rate, less leisure time*
  They say money is the root of all evil. Allowing greed to take control of your life could cause major issues, some of which are irreversible. Chasing money could cause you to uproot your foundation, neglect family and friends, and even miss irreplaceable moments that you can never get back. Ultimately, finding a balance is up to you, so make informed decisions.

- **Personal Experience:** I was able to land a decent job in my career field upon completion of college. I worked for a high-end retailer. This afforded me the opportunity to experience a company I had never been exposed to before. I was interacting with high-end clients such as professional athletes, attorneys, and financial advisors. While initially the job was fun and exciting, I knew I wanted more out of life than my current situation. Being around individuals like that all day does one of two things to you. Either it stokes your competitive spirit and challenges you to find your greatness, or it confirms their greatness and allows you to put them higher up on a pedestal than they already are in your mind.

  My job relocated me to Charlotte, North Carolina, a place undergoing rapid growth and change. What did this mean? It meant that there was plenty of opportunity for a rewarding career. The first thing I needed to do was identify my goals and then rack and stack them in order of importance. Once I completed this task, I realized that I was not on a path to accomplishing the goals that I had set out for myself in my earlier years.

  Eventually, I decided to make a change, and the United States military seemed at the time to be the answer to my questions. While increasing my income was one goal, it was not my only goal. Traveling the world was also a pretty high priority on my to-do list since I had never been outside of the United States. After doing some self-reflecting, I organized my life priorities. My top three priorities in life during this time were traveling, adventure, and money, in that order. After months of research and seeking wise counsel, I decided to join the military.

I figured I would be on the move a lot, so monitoring my expenses would become a priority. Purchases like a house or a new car just didn't seem smart to me. I even went as far as selling the old SUV I owned. Why sell a car that you own already? Well, after finding out my military situation and that my unit would have me on the move, it didn't make sense to have a vehicle that I barely drove. It also was on the older side; my mom had passed it down to me when I was on the way to college. It would soon be time for a new vehicle, so I figured I could sell it while it was running and in decent condition. It seemed like the logical move to me. My sibling had an extra vehicle that he was not using, so I was lucky enough to use his vehicle when I was in the States or required travel for my job. By taking this route, I was able to travel, get plenty of adventure, and drastically increase my income as I was never really around to spend any of it.

Thinking about something and having that thought come to fruition are two totally different things. After a few months of mostly saving, I took a glimpse at my account and immediately knew that I was onto something. I was increasing my income by eliminating, under normal conditions what most people consider necessities. Over the next year and a half, I went on to save approximately $25,000. It was at that point that I realized that I had become addicted to running up the bag. So, I continued to do just that for another year and a half.

As stated earlier, one plus one equals two, but two minus zero gives you the same results. My zero came in the form of paid travel, so I was able to minimize my expenses. I want to reiterate that you can never follow someone else's path. The reason this is not possible is that your path is like your fingerprint. It is unique to each individual person. None of us has any idea of the assistance, advantages, or even obstacles that particular person had along the way. So be wary of people who state they somehow followed in someone else's footsteps. I like to think that I am a straight shooter, so I will tell you flat out that it's a lie. Someone may give a blueprint and you can take that road as long as your situation allows you to but make your own destiny. My path worked for me because the timing was right for my situation. Your vision and your path must stay aligned. Even when you don't see progress, as long as your vision and path are aligned, you are right where you need to be, and you can make minor adjustments to correct any deficiencies.

"You can make money two ways—make more, or spend less."

—John Hope Bryant

CHAPTER 2

Minimizing the Outflow

While there are multiple ways to suppress spending in the urban and black communities, I figured what better way to start than with the biggest expense—housing expenditures! According to the US Bureau of Labor Statistics, housing in the African American community can be broken up into two categories: low- and high-income homes (Noël). I believe that there is always a middle class, but for the sake of argument, we will stick with these two categories. Higher-income families' housing expenses accounted for 34.2 percent of their annual income, whereas low-income families' expenses were nearly half their annual expenses, at 45.5 percent.

While I understand that everyone needs adequate shelter from the elements, I also find it unnecessary to lose your right arm doing so. I do not want to sound insensitive to anyone's situation because you must do what is necessary to survive. Buying a home requires a person to have a few different things working in their favor at the time of purchase. It requires credit, liquid cash, time, and even some level of financial literacy. Let's say we have a two-bedroom apartment available for rent for $950 per month and a three-bedroom home available for purchase for $850 per month. You would think that this decision would be easy. I know what you are thinking—well, duh! Everyone would pick the house because it is bigger and cheaper. Well, that is not completely the case according the statistics referenced later in this chapter.

Other factors like maintenance and location do play a role, but at some point, the math has to come into play. I get there are disadvantages to owning a home, like personal responsibility for maintenance, lawn care, and even homeowner's insurance. But the fact that you could potentially save $1,200 per year with the difference between the apartment and the home must count for something. If you must rent, then why not have more freedom and space and spend less money doing it? It should be acknowledged on the most basic of levels that a person buying a home does not necessarily have more money than a person who rents. Even though it may appear that way, looks can be deceiving. I will explain how and where it changes the game. The difference is that homeowners typically spend less per month by using someone else's money. In return, an agreement is made to stay for a specific amount of time in that same location.

Let's say a family is purchasing a $65,000 three-bedroom home on a fifteen-year mortgage at 5 percent with no money down. The monthly mortgage payment would be approximately $514.00. Now let's take that same family and put them in a three-bedroom apartment at $950.00 per month. Over the life of the loan for the house, they would pay a total of $92,520. This is broken down in detail below. After renting that apartment for fifteen years, the family's total would be $171,000. This family could almost pay for that house twice for the price of an apartment while investing for the same amount of time.

Let's say that our family is a family of four, with Mom, Dad, and two children. They could do a lot of things with that money difference saved between the apartment and the home ($78,480 over fifteen years). The parents could use that money to purchase new cars or make additions to the home. As an alternative the parents could fully fund one of the kids' college tuition. If they are lucky enough to have two kids going to college, they could pay for three-quarters of both their children's college tuition from the savings of purchasing versus renting. This is where that phrase "slow and steady wins the race" comes into play. This is just one of the many ways that the rich continue to widen the already enormous economic gap between themselves and everybody else.

Home: $514 x 12 months = $6,168
$6,168 x 15 years = $92,520
$64,998 principal + $27,522 interest = $92,520 total loan cost

Apartment: $950 x 12 months = $11,400
$11,400 x 15 years = $171,000
$171,000 - $92,520 = $78,480

If you forecast your housing expenses and remain disciplined, then you give yourself a great shot at accomplishing your goals. This should make purchasing a home a little bit more desirable. Even if you don't purchase a home, in most markets renting a home is more financially beneficial than renting an apartment in the long run. I do understand whom I am talking to, and most people in their early to mid-twenties are not really all that interested in buying a home. This next section is for my eighteen- to thirty-year-old readers.

The goal is to absolutely reduce the amount of money spent. Buying versus renting is not the only way to reduce housing expenses. Staying home or moving back in with your support system is my favorite way to minimize the outflow of cash. If the method is not abused and is used correctly, it is the most efficient way to build your account. I assume you want to know why this is my favorite method. Well, it is actually pretty simple. I wholeheartedly believe in the team concept. I love to reference teachings from my days in organized sports and apply them to current life situations. Unless you stay under a huge rock, I am sure that you have heard the phrase "two heads are better than one." Steph Curry and the Warriors often use the phrase "strength in numbers."

Both phrases and many more like them are simply stating the obvious. The more like-minded people you have surrounding you, the greater chance you have of succeeding.

Staying home, moving back in with your parents, or even getting a roommate all have different benefits. While moving in with a roommate is a good option, it is not the best. For that reason, we will not go into detail about it because it is self-explanatory.

Let us start with staying home. For this example, we will assume that the people who stay home do not go to college but go straight into the workforce after high school. On the other hand, we will assume that the people moving back in with their parents are college graduates. I am aware that there are plenty of people who stay home and attend college, but the vast majority leave home in some manner. Staying in the house can be super annoying after dealing with your parents for eighteen years. I was eighteen as well, so trust me, I get it. However, the truth is society has scammed us into believing eighteen is the standard to be pushed out on your own. To put it nicely, a young adult doesn't know anything about the world or how it operates. To the parents, they will fail; and when they fail, then what? Then the parent must go bail them out of whatever jam they may be in. Most of the time, the mistake is more costly than just teaching them the correct ways and methods from the beginning. So, if you really think about it, nobody wins if the children are not prepared. If you are lucky enough to have the opportunity to stay home, I am advising you to stay as long as you can. Doing so will help prepare you for your financial freedom and potentially save your parents a boatload of cash in the process. This is where the team concept comes into play again.

We will revisit our family of four again, but this time we're going to name them. The parents will be Mr. and Mrs. Jenkins, and the two siblings will be named Steve and Alexis. For scenario purposes, this is a middle-class family with two kids struggling to get by. Steve has a full-time job since graduating high school. Steve and his parents reached an agreement that if he stayed home, he would assume responsibility for his car insurance, cable, and cell phone bill. Steve's bills total $275: $100 cable, $100 cell phone, and $75 car insurance. With a full-time job paying $8.50 per hour, Steve makes enough money to cover all his bills out of one weekly check. All these monthly expenses are expenses that would have been incurred no matter his location. Being able to save three checks per month is a win for Steve. The Jenkins parents are also winning by getting an additional $275 per month that they had not been receiving before Steve was working.

$$\$275 \times 12 \text{ months} = \$3,300$$

The extra funds that are now being received by the parents can be used for a variety of things. Paying some of the interest down on the home, going on a much-needed vacation, or even buying Alexis a car for college are just a few ways the extra money can be used. The team is now $3,300 stronger per year. More importantly they all have the opportunity to increase their accounts in some way because Steve is now circulating more money through the team. I have always believed that if my mom has money, then I will always have money, and vice versa. That is just the way a team should work.

After surveying several individuals who either stayed home, moved back in, or got their own place, I found the two variables that were consistently mentioned were more money and more freedom. Now personally, I can tell you that having freedom and being broke isn't really freedom at all. You are still confined, either by your space or financial circumstances. If Steve maintains this for a few years, he will be able to experience things that his counterparts from the inner city and even the country seldom gets to experience. Steve could possibly take a trip to Africa, open his own business, or even purchase a condominium by the age of twenty-four.

Moving back in with Mom and Dad after college will be a huge adjustment. You would be giving up all the freedoms that you were once used to. This is an experience that, unlike your counterparts who never left home, you have tasted—sweet freedom! Moving back in with the folks means no more boyfriends sleeping over and no more walking around naked. Hell, it probably means no more doing the oochie coochie. While the privacy and personal freedoms of college are great, the young adult who decided to stay home has the potential to have a fat account with little to no debt. That is a trade-off that, if given the opportunity, most people would kill for. This means people like Steve may have more disposable income even though a college graduate makes more money.

Everyone is forced to figure out life after graduation. For some, student loan debt, combined with working an entry-level position that really doesn't care about your degree at all, will make you seriously question your life decisions. If you have the support, the first thing you should do is move back in with your parents or some established relative. Most parents by the time you graduate are in their early to mid-fifties. As my younger cousin always says, "they got it," i.e. they probably have a lot more disposable income by that age, especially depending on the number of children left in the house. If they purchased a home when they were young, it is close to, if not completely, paid off. Looking back a few paragraphs ago, remember that housing totals at least approximately a third of the black community's expenditures. If you are lucky to have financially sound parents, they may even be cashing in bonds. What is the point to all this? Well, the point is, unless you still have younger siblings in the house, your parents or guardians may have little to no monthly expenditures. What does that mean for Alexis? It means that her parents probably won't require much because they are financially stable.

As a college graduate, you probably had the unfortunate pleasure of paying someone rent. So even if your parents ask you for $400 per month, you know how big a win this is. Why is it a win? Because even though you lose freedom, for $400 a month, you gain home-cooked meals, cable, water, lights, and even the occasional Saturday morning car wash from Dad if you are a female. For the guys, nobody does your laundry and folds your clothes like Mom. If you know where you can find all this for $400 dollars, then let me know because I want to move there now.

For our second scenario, we have a young lady named Ashley who graduated college recently. If Ashley placed herself on a three-year plan to stay with her parents after graduation, when her time comes, she could put herself in a great position to make whatever financial moves are needed. For example, let us assume that Ashley has a full-time job making $33k per year. She accumulated $25K in student loan debt. If she is a responsible young lady, then she can pay off her student loan debt during her three-year stay with her parents. Additionally, over the course of that same three-year period, Ashley should be able to save at least $30,000. Unless you are rich, having a running account balance of $30K puts you way above most Americans in their late twenties. So, when you hear someone talking bad about moving in or staying with your parents for a while, forgive them because that means they don't understand the complete concept of a team. You eat, I eat, and we eat.

Buying power is the single greatest asset that my people possess today. The urban community, but more specifically African Americans, spend an obscene amount of money consuming a variety of products each year. With more famous athletes and performers than any other ethnic group on earth, it's not a surprise that our purchasing power has reached one trillion dollars annually (Brian). Now I do not want to discredit all the entrepreneurs, doctors, attorneys, politicians, Fortune 500 executives, and scientists that we have in our communities. By the way, we have never had more at any other point in our history than we do right now. Couple that with our impressive African American queens, who are consuming degrees at a high rate. In fact, that rate is so high that, according to multiple sources, black women earned more degrees by percentage than any other group, including white men and women, over the past few years (Helm Bronner). Even with all that being said, people will still naturally gravitate to athletes and entertainers. If the person looks like you, then the publics level of interest tends to be magnified. The problem with this is Russell Westbrook, 2 Chainz, and Kerry Washington are usually being paid to wear designer stuff, but you, my friend, are not. While we may think we are supporting our people because we are wearing the brand, in actuality you really are not supporting them unless they own the clothing line. When 2 Chainz does a toy drive in Atlanta or pays a single mother's rent for a year, those things are more likely done using his own dime. I am 100 percent positive that Gucci is not investing in Columbia's, Charlotte's, or Atlanta's inner-city project housing or giving those kids free shoes for any sort of back-to-school bash. Why? Well, it can be attributed to multiple reasons, but most importantly it is because the inner city is not their desired target market. For the company, it is considered free market share. What is free market share? It is simply unplanned publicity. Even though 2Chainz may be from the inner city, he does not only have fans from the inner city. He is also enjoyed by Black Ivy League graduates, rich Asian Americans, poor Caucasian kids, and middle-class Hispanics. A company like Gucci is after the upper middle class and lower upper-class fans of the rapper.

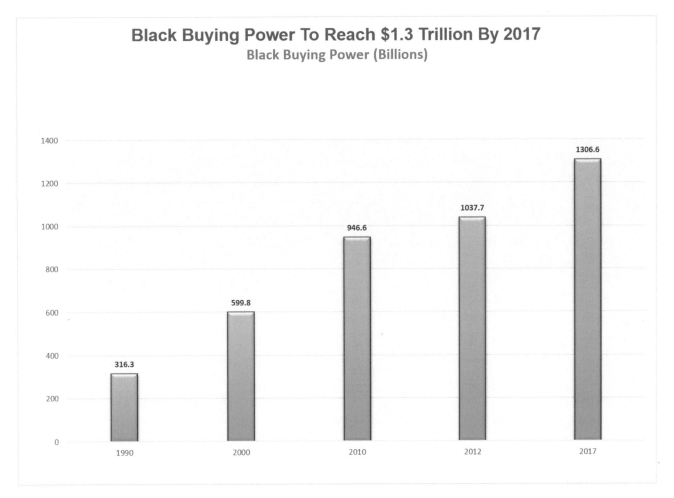

Black Buying Power To Reach $1.3 Trillion By 2017

Black Buying Power (Billions)

While I am not shocked by the steady growth of black purchasing power and I should not be shocked by the length of time that the dollar circulates through our community, I am. After reading a report done by the NAACP, you should be just as shocked and embarrassed as I am. The report states, "Currently, a dollar circulates in Asian communities for a month, in Jewish communities approximately 20 days, and White communities 17 days. How long does a dollar circulate in the Black community? 6 hours!!! African American buying power is at 1.1 trillion; and yet only 2 cents of every dollar an African American spends in this country goes back to Black owned business" (Thaii).

Now by no means am I telling you to only purchase from black businesses. I am strictly against purchasing unnecessary items. But if you are going to buy things that you don't need, then you may want to do so from people who will invest it back into your community. At least that way you get some sort of return on value for your money spent. Even with that being said, I still understand that money is the most effective way to promote change. In today's society, if you shut off the revenue source of a person, one of two things will happen: they will either conform to your desires, or they will attack you because you are threatening their livelihood.

There are a million ways to cut back on money spent on everyday purchases. As referenced earlier in the book, maintaining situational awareness is paramount. As you know, not every cheap thing is good; you often get what you pay for. Eating out may be one of the most underrated bills that we accumulate. For all you non-cookers, aka foodies, you are creating one hell of a bill. Preparing your food at home is not only healthier but usually substantially cheaper over the course of a week, a month, or even a year. Consider how much you spend on food. For this scenario we are going to price a good salad at $10. Now let's say you are a person like me who loves a variety of different things on your salad: eggs, croutons, cheese, cucumbers, olives, peppers, and maybe some almonds. Add that to the cost of the salad, and you are looking at about a $13 meal. In the grocery store, $13 can almost get you everything to create a salad and have two to three servings of that same salad.

I cannot forget about my fast-food lovers. You are really blowing up a check eating at these places daily. A good meal at an established fast-food restaurant will run you approximately $7. Can we agree that a realistic number for weekly fast-food meals on average is four or five? Now if we can agree, you calculate and tell me how much money you are spending daily. Again, that is under the assumption that four or five is normal. I could go on about this forever, but at the end of the day, it is self-explanatory that preparing your food in the comfort of your home could save you big dollars.

I could not have a chapter about limiting your spending without talking about shopping. Ladies and gentlemen, this should be evident after seeing those staggering statistics earlier in the chapter. I will elaborate more on spending habits in the personal experience section of this chapter, but the bottom line is stop consuming things you don't need.

Another way to save some major coins is by putting yourself on a club diet. To be clear, when I say club, I don't mean the sandwich. I know, you probably never quite heard it phrased that way, but that could be exactly what you need. It is not a secret to anyone in the urban community that clubs can be extremely expensive if done in excess. This is a part of our culture, as we love dancing, socializing, and getting lit. The reasons why are an entirely different conversation for another day, but I will tell you that if you are of African lineage, you didn't steal it. Your ancestors celebrated a lot back in the motherland. I recommend pulling back altogether from partying for a while, but that takes a different type of discipline. So, if you must party, then find a cheaper way to scratch your itch. For all my readers who attended college at one point, you should remember this amazing thing called a house party. *Find one!* For my readers who have not yet gone to college, I will let you in on a secret. When you are broke, house parties will be the best thing since sliced bread to you. They are usually free: you can socialize, drink, and pick up your future MCM or WCW. If you are past the college stage, then find a bar. Now the drinks are not free, but you still should be able to socialize and find your potential wife in the bar. Okay, I am just kidding about finding your wife in the bar. A bar isn't the most ideal place to bag your future wife, but crazier things have happened. Again, I recommend taking a break altogether from partying when you are practicing smart spending, but if you must party, then do it in moderation.

Now the final way to minimize your cash flow is to manage your student loan debt if you have any. I am touching on this, but I will not elaborate. My suggestion is that individuals with this debt do some research about loan consolidation. This is just one of the many ways to manage your debt by lowering your monthly payments and maybe even your overall debt. Also, certain jobs qualify for the federal loan forgiveness program. This too is another avenue to wipe out or put a serious dent in the student loan debt.

- **Pros of Minimizing Your Outflow:** *larger account balance, more closet space, potential of eliminating small debt, and more importantly, having the means to grow the team and their assets*

  Minimizing your spending will benefit you, but it does not only have to be about you. Your community, area, and culture could all benefit from your financial liberation. Just as importantly, your immediate team could also increase their assets. Remember that the stronger the team, the better your chances of winning.

- **Cons of Minimizing Your Outflow:** *being out of the social loop, lacking the latest retail, a loss of personal space and maybe even freedom*

  Moving back in with your parents, not being seen, or even shopping less is not the vision you had of how you would spend your twenties. However, I am sure you didn't envision being broke either. Not being able to take trips and buy nice things in your thirties and forties must be terrible. So, either you can do more with less in your twenties or do more with more in your thirties. By this time, you should be on the road to becoming established in your career, which means you should be making more money. Don't let societal pressures deter you from gaining financial stability and economic dominance over your debt.

- **Personal Experience:** There is a misconception that women are the only ones with bad shopping habits. While I would agree that most women I know own a million pairs of heels, this fashion forward world is also filled with guys who own an unnecessary number of suits, shoes, and accessories. Now I know that women will not like what I am about to propose, but this is for the best. I put myself on a store diet. For one year I was only allowed to shop in TJ Maxx on the clearance rack, and I could not purchase any sneakers or Cole Haans. (By the way, this became my bad habit a few years back, which I will discuss later.) Keep in mind the situational awareness rule. If neither of these apply, then find out what does and fill in the blank. For all you sneakerheads, this will no doubt be rough. The same could be said to my ladies who love their heels.

This took a lot of discipline on my end because at the time, I was still wearing J's. The first few months, I didn't purchase any shoes. You would think that was the plan, right? Wrong! The plan was to starve myself of the things I unnecessarily consumed most. Not buying sneakers the first few months was out of sheer stubbornness. But then something remarkable happened to me after the third month. I began to develop a taste for other shoes. Plus, I started realizing that I could no longer wear sneakers as often as I could when I was back in high school and college. My job required specific attire, so my shoes were only being worn on rainy days and weekends.

The TJ Maxx struggle was a little different, even though I had previously shopped at the store and really liked the merchandise. I usually only went there for specific items. Now that I was forced to purchase my clothes from their racks, it required a different level of browsing. I was now noticing articles of clothing that I had not given the time of day before. It is always good to expand your horizons, no matter the means of doing so. Shopping on the clearance rack cut my cost by more than half. By the time I knew it, I was in the month of December, and I had saved myself hundreds of dollars. This task that felt so difficult at the beginning had now become easy money in my pocket.

Between the shoes, clothes, and being loyal to specific brands, I was being hustled out of my money for a long time, and this is coming from a person who studied supply and demand in college and who thoroughly understands it. This experiment caused my pockets to fatten, my wardrobe to become more diverse, and me to low-key have a new favorite store. Identify your bad spending habits, and don't be afraid to attack them. Don't fool yourself into thinking you can eliminate them, but minimizing them is possible. Ladies may have a real beef with not purchasing heels for a year, but the risk here is definitely worth the reward. Again, to all you sneakerheads, not buying may feel like death initially but once you start to realize how much extra money you have, then I am almost positive you will change your tune.

"Think of money like a bike. If a child with three friends is given a bike and then hands over that bike to someone he doesn't even know, the bike may disappear forever. But if he gives that bike to one of his three friends, each of these friends can give the bike to each other over and over again, and will therefore always have a ride. Money is not intended to be short-lived and perishable commodity. It is meant to be used over and over again."

—Dr. Boyce Watkins, PhD

CHAPTER 3

Leverage

Leverage: (verb) to use for gain, exploit. Everyone has an opinion about credit—good, bad, or comme ci, comme ça (so-so in French). Everything in life has more than one purpose. Anything, if abused, can cause serious harm. I will not dive deeply into credit as it can become very complex and I still have much to learn. I can, however, give you the basics in hopes that it jump-starts your financial train. Before we get into the different avenues of credit, let's nip this in the bud right now. Credit is the way of the world and is here to stay. We did not create credit, and we sure as hell won't destroy it. The next move is learning how to manipulate it to our advantage.

There are multiple loans that fall under the credit umbrella. When you think of credit, usually credit cards come to mind, but credit has multiple lending methods. There are credit cards, automobile loans, housing loans, and even the dreaded student loans. These are all forms of credit that can be borrowed against your name. I will elaborate on credit cards since they are the most frequently used and usually the smallest of the bunch.

You have your pick of two types of credit cards, secured and unsecured. The secured card is my recommendation for anyone who is on a tight budget. This card builds confidence and can give you an idea of how credit cards work. "Secured" simply means that the card has some sort of collateral against it, usually in the form of cash. An unsecured card has no collateral associated with it. The difference between the two is simple. The two remind me of cell phone plans. A secured card would be like a prepaid phone—you only spend what you load. The unsecured card allows you to spend or talk until they shut you off for going over your minutes. Why do I like the secured credit card so much? Well, if you are on a tight budget while attempting to get your first credit card, then it is likely that you cannot afford an unsecured card. This does not apply to everyone, but this is where being real with yourself comes into play. Hey, I can totally relate! Trust me, I had many days during college where my account was tight.

As I stated earlier, using your own money as collateral allows you to have a predetermined credit limit. This is, in my opinion, the best way for a beginner to learn how credit cards work. If everything in your financial life started to fall apart, one thing you would not have to worry about is the secured card. Why? Because the bank already has your money. If you start defaulting on your loan, the bank takes your money and pays the credit card bill for you. While I recommend secured cards for beginners, I do not want to confuse any of my readers. An unsecured card is absolutely the goal of this entire chapter. You gain the most leverage by using someone else's money, while keeping yours available. This is how the rich stay rich.

I will let you in on a secret: rich people don't like using their own money. Back to secured cards, though. I believe for starters that the smaller the amount, the better the chance of the new cardholder not abusing the card. The secured number for me was $500, but we will get into that in the personal experience section. It's not like the new cardholder with a small balance will be treating all their friends to a Vegas trip or anything. So, for that reason alone, it is very good for beginners. You can purchase things like gas, groceries, and maybe even pay for a fancy dinner date somewhere. Obviously, the card must be used in moderation. The card will benefit you if and only if you can show the company a responsible spending pattern. Remember that they want to lend **y**ou money, because the more you borrow, the more they make.

Credit cards have a magic percentage that if not surpassed, supposedly increases your credit if all payments are made on time. This is debatable and has been for a long time. Everyone has what they think is the magic percentage. Most places will tell you that 30 percent is the standard. For consistency purposes, we are going with 30 percent. This is a good starting point for a few different reasons. First, credit card companies respond better to you when you don't spend all your money. Why? They do this because maxing out a card makes you look like a financial liability. The second reason is because 30 percent is a hell of a lot easier to pay off than 80 percent. I also want to be clear in saying you can spend more than the magic percentage number, but I would not recommend it. Once you are a little more seasoned and have built your credit up to a respectable score, then you may be okay to start pushing the envelope. Knowing that the card companies respond well if card utilization is between 0 to 30 percent gives you something to strive for. Depending on the credit card limit, you may not be able to make many purchases.

$$500 \times 30\% = \$150$$

Depending on your situation, $150 might be able to cover gas and groceries for one month. The secured card, like anything else, has its drawbacks. The fees associated with this card are typically higher. The bank knows that you are at a disadvantage. The lenders view secured cardholders as a higher risk to default on their loans. This is primarily due to the cardholder's lack of borrowing history. Nevertheless, you can believe that the bank is looking to profit from this. Paying higher interest is never a good thing, which is why this card is only a springboard to build your credit.

Once you have obtained the card, how do you make it work to your advantage? Well for starters, you do not have to pay the full amount every month. I just wanted to throw that out there because this is a common misconception about credit cards. With that being said, you should never pay just the minimum either. If you start down this road, then you are adopting bad financial habits. You will also be setting yourself up to pay a lot more money over the life of the card. Remember, the goal of leveraging money is using as much of someone else's stuff as you need, while paying them back as little as you can. Interest adds up over time, and if you do not have a handle on it, you could be just giving the bank unnecessary money.

Do not allow interest to pin you into a corner. If you do, I promise you this will be a game that you lose. Keep in mind that the amount spent matters, but not as much as the credit history. Also, keep that percentage in the back of your mind. If you do, you'll be well on your way to a 760-credit score in no time.

Last, I would like to leave you with things that credit scores can affect. If you recall the housing story in chapter 2, then you should remember the substantial amount of money that can be saved over time if you own versus rent. A home will probably be most people's biggest investment, unless they own a business. That lovely home that you are going to purchase will be with credit. A very small percentage of people will pay $200K in cash for a home. One reason a lot of African Americans in the inner city rent apartments instead of purchasing homes is because they do not have credit. Credit was not a real topic of conversation in my community when I was growing up, other than the occasional "you need to have good credit." But this is not the conversation that will help you understand or obtain credit. In other communities they have those conversations with their children all the time because they understand the importance better than we do for a slew of different reasons. Well, all that stops here. The secret is out, and you should want in.

- **Pros to Using Leverage:** *access to purchase more, better prepared for emergencies, building credit history, gaining an understanding of how credit works and using the knowledge to your advantage in order to benefit your family for decades to come*

  As stated above, credit can be a benefit for the future. Start seeing the bigger picture. You need to ask yourself not only how can this benefit me now, but how can it benefit me in fifteen years? Whether we are speaking about multiple homes, businesses, vehicles, or even vessels, all these items, if used properly, can increase your net worth. More importantly, these are all things that can be passed down from generation to generation. Why spend $200K up front when you can break that up over twenty years?

- **Cons to Using Leverage:** *paying more money than you borrowed (interest), easy financial trap if you spend more than you can afford to pay, potential to shop more frequently as you have access to more money*

  Discipline is the key to making credit work for you. Spending more money goes against the initial goal of this book, but you also must understand your situation. Scared money doesn't make any money. Having to pay a little interest now for a bigger line of credit later sounds like it's worth it to me. Only you can be the judge of that, but just make sure if you do it, you have a plan set in place. As long as you have one and stick to it, manipulating this credit thing won't be as foreign as it once was.

- **Personal Experience:** I increased my credit score, but between me and you, I had no idea what I was doing. I really did not have any sort of plan because at the time I didn't understand credit that well. When I was twenty years old, I attempted to get my first credit card and got denied. I was super embarrassed about getting rejected because when it happened, I was with my homeboy Travis, and he got approved. Over the next year or so, I went on to try again and got denied by every retail store you could think of. (Again, not understanding how credit works can hinder your progression.) At this point it was no longer about the card but more about my pride. After that year was up, I gave up trying to get a credit card for about three years. Fast-forward to my twenty-fourth birthday, when I decided it was time to be an adult and get, or at least try to get, a credit card. I had a lot more confidence this time around as I had educated myself on credit and how things work.

I went to my bank and set up a secured credit card in my name. I previously ran my credit score before opening the card and found out that I had a score of 560. While terrible, in retrospect it wasn't that bad because I did not have a credit history. They approved me for a secured card with a credit limit of $500. I told myself that I would only use it for emergencies, gas, and groceries. The bank representative told me to keep the card for a year and then increase my limit. I ended up using the card for almost three years and never increased my limit. I never really saw a need to increase it because the card was living up to its potential. While this was not a planned move, it was the best move for me. Because the credit limit was small, I was able to set up an automatic payment every month, which ensured that I would never miss a payment. I seldom went over that magic percentage number, but when that happened, I was able to make a bigger monthly payment.

After using the card faithfully for about three years, I started having all kinds of credit card companies writing me. The credit limits started out slightly higher than my current balance, but then they started getting ridiculous. I started seeing numbers like $10,000 and $15,000. By this time, I was aware of the power that I possessed and told myself: "Well, if they offered me $15K, then I can get $30K." I knew my credit score had increased, but because I wasn't pressed, I never cared to check it. I told myself that I would throw every letter in the trash until one came with $50K plus on it. I finally decided to check my score, and after three and a half years, it blew my mind. My credit score went from 560 and my not being able to get a credit card anywhere, to 796 and receiving offers in the mail for credit limits over $30K. The card companies continued to write, and the amounts continued to grow exponentially. At age twenty-four, I had to settle for a $500 secured card. At age twenty-seven, credit card companies were trying to give me over $50,000 unsecured.

Again, I cannot pretend that this was the plan every step of the way. But I did have an understanding and a plan of how to get to my desired destination. I was disciplined enough to stay at $500, not listen to the bank representative, and not be pressed about increasing my limit. So many times, we take more because we can, but that is not always what's best. I stayed dedicated to making monthly payments, and I seldom topped that magic percentage. While three years is a long time, I also know that a score going up over 230 points is a huge deal. Remember that my path may not be your path, but you can hopefully take something from my lessons and apply it to your situation.

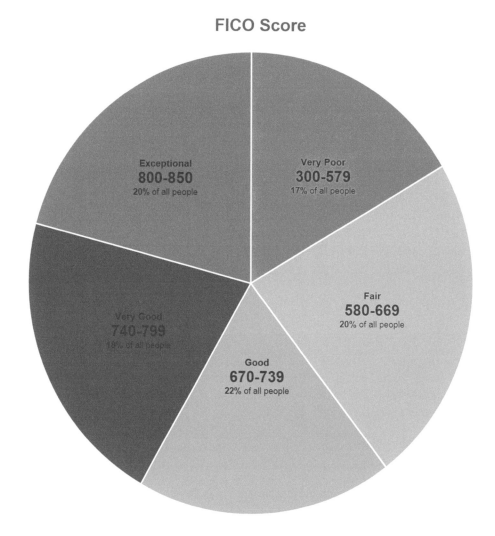

FICO Score

Very Poor
300-579
17% of all people

Fair
580-669
20% of all people

Good
670-739
22% of all people

Very Good
740-799
18% of all people

Exceptional
800-850
20% of all people

Vantage Score

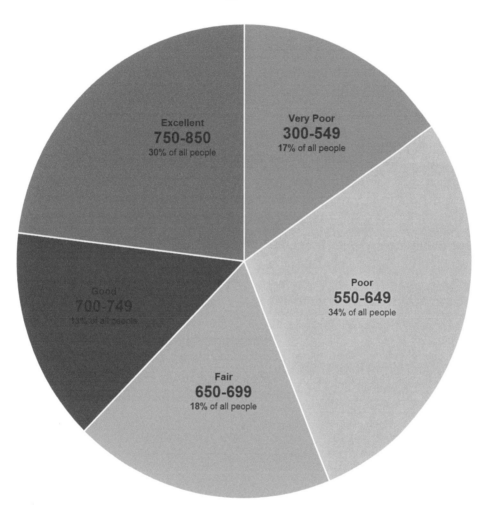

Excellent
750-850
30% of all people

Very Poor
300-549
17% of all people

Poor
550-649
34% of all people

Good
700-749
13% of all people

Fair
650-699
18% of all people

"You wanna know what's more important than throwing money away in the strip club…………Credit."

—Jay-Z (Shawn Carter), *4:44* Album (2017)

CHAPTER 4

Investments

It may sound a little ironic that you are reading about how to save and stretch the dollar, yet I am telling you to invest. Once upon a time, they were separate thoughts, not to be mentioned in the same sentence. Well, those days are long gone. The wealthy, rich, and ambitious people in the world tie the two together like a shoestring.

The million-dollar question is always "What do I invest in?" The truth of the matter is that the people who really know the answer to that question don't want you to know. A lot of people who pretend to know only tell you for their own financial gain. You also have those people who are shooting in the dark and learning on the fly, but I will give credit where credit is due. Shooting in the dark may be risky but it is still better than not shooting at all.

The urban community, which is mostly made up of Hispanics and African Americans, by and large has not traditionally participated in the stock market. This has not been statistically measured and proven, but I would dare to say that more minorities own Apple iPhones than we do stocks in America. According to an article by the Nielsen Company, "Asian/Pacific Islanders (86.6%), Black-African American (83%), and Hispanics (82.4%) are the top three groups with the highest rates of smartphone ownership, compared with 74.2% of non-Hispanic whites." The same article went on to state "Apple, meanwhile, remained the top smartphone manufacturer, with 43.6% of mobile subscribers in the U.S. owning an iPhone." Unfortunately, I am willing to bet that we do not have north of 43 percent stock ownership as a people.

For those of you who are not math geniuses, don't feel bad I need a calculator as well. There are approximately 46.3 million African Americans in the United States. If you take 83 percent and multiply it times the African American population, you get roughly 38 million. Of that 38 million, 43 percent own iPhones, which would mean approximately 16 million African Americans own iPhones. That means that more than 16 million people in our community would have to actively participate in the stock market to be equal. Yeah, right! Once you stop and think, it is really sad, because we are financially behind the eight ball and playing catchup. We cannot afford to do the same things that other ethnic groups are doing. We must be smarter and better in order to close the gap. Hey, I FaceTime a lot and I like my iPhone just as much as the next person, so I am not telling you that you shouldn't purchase one. I am simply saying your creation and consumption of wealth should never be equal. Just in case I am not being clear enough, what you spend should never come close to what you make.

I want this book to spark light bulbs in every type of thinker. If the stock market has shown a steady financial gain and no one is being hurt, harmed, or endangered, would you not want in on that? News flash: most of the goods and services in America are produced by whites. So, does that mean that it is okay to spend your money and make them rich but not invest and get rich with them? I would like to know if and when someone finds logic in not investing. If you do, please let me know because risks are associated with everything in life, including breathing. So, back to investing. You can invest your money into so many different things that it will give you a headache thinking about it. I will list the four that, in my opinion, require you to break down your investing into two categories, short- and long-term investments. You have ETFs, mutual funds, stocks, and real estate.

I will start with ETFs and mutual funds. Some may argue that the order of my list is interchangeable, and that's okay because no way is this list set in stone. For me, both fall under short-term investments because they tend to move slightly faster than the other two. Remember that this is a basic introduction to the world of investing and will most definitely require more research by you. ETFs (exchange-traded funds) are similar to common stock. ETFs experience price changes daily as they are bought and sold. They also typically have a higher daily liquidity, which makes them more attractive. Don't let the fancy terms scare you. This simply means that trading them is better because the value of the asset doesn't go down as easily.

Mutual funds are an investment that enables investors to pool their money together. Mutual funds are cool because they allow you to invest in stocks, bonds, cash, or a combination of these assets. This is specifically important for beginners because this option allows you to get into investing and does not require as much knowledge as some of the other options. Both ETFs and mutual funds typically have a shorter shelf life, but both can be beneficial in their own right. Long-term investments would be considered things like stocks and real estate. These two types of investments are held on to for a long time.

What is a stock? A stock is a security that signifies ownership in a corporation. More importantly, this allows for the stockholder to claim part of the corporation's assets or earnings. Let's break this down to its most basic level. Mario can choose a company, pay money to buy into that company, and the better the company does, the more money Mario makes because he owns shares in the company. As they say in the Army, "Too Easy." Hell yeah, I want Nike to pay me because I pay them every time I buy some kicks. Damn right Wal-Mart owes me money, as much stuff as I purchased from them in college. These are all things that should be going through your head after reading this if they are not already.

Finally, we have real estate. This is probably the most recognizable form of long-term investing. What is real estate? Real estate is a piece of property consisting of land or a building. If you are American, you were taught this at a very young age, but maybe your teachers didn't elaborate enough. Just like the game Monopoly, the world has a scarcity of space, which means that there's only so much. The more you buy, the greater the chance that someone will land on your Pennsylvania Avenue and have to pay you $390.00 per stop. Real estate can have so many different benefits, whether it is keeping property for your family, quick selling, or renting it for a steady stream of income. I remember when one of my mentors introduced me to stocks. He was telling me his story about Apple and saying how long he had owned shares. He told me that he had owned shares in the company before he owned his home.

No matter what avenue of investing you choose to go down, just make sure that you are doing your research and picking the right option for you. Of course, investing requires money, but even if money is tight, that is still no excuse not to invest. Having a spending plan can save you a few dollars here and there. We will discuss this in more detail in later chapters. There is no such thing as too small an investment. If I remember correctly Bitcoin cost $0.60 in 2010, and now it is currently over 10K. So, investing $25 in the right thing at the right time can make you rich.

Saving money is only good for two things: emergency funds, which we will discuss later in the book, and investments. Why else would any sane person allow the thing you work for every single day to sit in someone else's possession for the majority of the year? I have yet to meet a financially savvy person who saves money to make money off the bank. Now they may take advantage of the interest from the bank while waiting on their opportunity, but nobody actually believes in that myth. How does it benefit you otherwise? Think of money like food. Between the exchange rate and inflation, your dollars have an expiration date. Allowing money to sit in the bank is like allowing food to sit in the refrigerator. It slowly starts to diminish. The longer you leave it in, the worse off it becomes. Below is a graph to give you an idea of just how much the banks are paying you for using your money.

Bank	Savings APY	APY Minimum Balance
Alley Bank	1.00%	$0
Bank of America	0.01%	$0
Barclays	1.00%-1.05%	$0
Capital One	0.75%	$0
Chase Bank	0.01%	$0
Citibank	0.01%	$0
Citizens Bank	0.01%-0.05%	$0
Fifth Third Bank	0.01%	$0.01
HSBC	0.01%	$0
Huntington National Bank	0.02%-0.05%	$0.01
KeyBank	0.01%-0.02%	$0.01-$0.02%
M&T Bank	0.02%	$1
PNC Bank	0.01%-0.03%	$0
Radius	0.05%	$50
Regions	0.01%	$0
SunTrust	0.01%	$0
Synchrony	1.05%	$0
TD Bank	0.05%	$0
US Bank	0.01%	$0
Wells Fargo	0.01%-0.03%	$0
Woodforest National Bank	0.05%	$0

Let's say the bank is paying .05%, and you have $2,000 in the bank. You will end up making approximately $1 for the entire year. So now the question becomes, "Would you allow a friend to borrow 2K for a year if they promised to pay you back $2,001?" I know if I had something better to do with my money, I wouldn't. Actually, even if I didn't have anything better to do with my money, I would not let someone hold my $2K for a year for $1! The risk isn't worth the reward.

In chapter 3, I said a home would be your biggest investment, which I still stand by, but there are always exceptions to the rule. For most, a home will be their largest investment, but for some, you are your biggest investment. Usually these investments are intangible, but you have the potential to pay more profit back than any stock. There are several ways to invest in yourself. Education usually is the first and biggest investment that comes to mind, but of course, there are others that don't cost as much but are just as important.

A balanced appearance is key. Typical hygiene is obviously important, but along with that comes your attire. Your hair shouldn't look like a celebrity stylist did it while your suit looks like you borrowed it from homeless Joe. Investing in the proper attire is just as much a part of your introduction as anything. This advice applies to both men and women. Purchasing a good suit can be very beneficial and versatile.

Why do I keep using the word *investing* versus *buying* when I am referencing suits and business attire? First impressions are important and could be the determining factor for professional and personal advancement. A good suit can be tailored to fit your size. Depending on the suit's color, it can be used as interchangeable pieces. The seasoned suit-wearing man or woman may tell you that's why sport coats and slacks were invented. Who cares what they say? They didn't pay for it, and hardly anyone will know the difference. You can wear a good suit three different ways. The jacket can be worn as a sport coat. The suit pants can be worn as slacks with a shirt and tie, or the entire suit can be worn when you have an important event coming up. I don't know of many small investments that pay dividends like owning a good suit. Remember that first impressions mean everything, but second and third ones are important too.

Now don't misunderstand what investing in a suit means. It does not mean you have to go purchase a Ralph Lauren suit for $2,200 when you're on a budget. You can shop around and find a bargain, but this is a necessary investment.

- **Pros to Investing:** *being able to retire with few to no financial worries, giving yourself the opportunity to get rich, building generational wealth, knowing your money is making you money while you are busy with life, opportunity to meet new like-minded people and expand your horizons*

  I'm sure you work very hard for your money, so to have it not work hard for you is crazy. I want to retire early and travel for a living just like the people in the movies. Well, that will not happen by simply working a job and putting your money in the bank. Seek financial help and make those same companies that you are paying pay you.

- **Cons to Investing:** *possibility of losing hard-earned money, requires more work or less leisure time, requires sacrificing of short-term income*

  Take your time and make sure that you seek financial advice before investing. If you are one of those do-it-yourself types of learners, then make sure you dedicate the time to reaching your investment avenue. Growing up I would hear the old men gambling, and they would always say,

"Scared money don't make no money, youngblood." It took me a while to understand how deep that was, but now I apply it to my everyday life.

- **Personal Experience:** Investing can be a great thing, but I would be remiss not to mention the negatives, if they are not something that is already evident to you. As an investor I have had some good days and obviously some bad ones. Any investor will tell you that losing is not the goal, but it comes with the territory. You will be fine as long as you win more than you lose, and if you are trying to get rich, then you need to consistently win more than you lose.

Investing can also become addictive, which is my current state of being. This can become dangerous when greed starts to cloud your judgment and decisions. I made some very hasty investment decisions that caused me to lose $5,000. Now while that isn't an excessive amount of money, it was huge to me, being one year removed from college. I have since learned from my mistakes and try to make better decisions. But all this talking needs to make sense to you, so I am going to break it down for you. Growing up no one ever really explained it to me this way. If they had, then I may have been rich by now, but I am going to give you what I didn't get. I can't tell you what to invest in, but I can show you how investing can be super addictive, profitable, and exciting.

I was talking to a friend of mine named Monique, and I was explaining to her how I felt as though I had been hustled out of my early twenties because I didn't really know much about investing. Let's take Amazon, for example, since this is one of the stocks that I own. From the image below, you can see that Amazon in 2016 was under $500 per share. For this example, we will say it was an even $480. For every $480 you paid, you owned one share of the company. If you look at the current value of the stock, one share is worth $1,515.93. Which means that over the past three years, seeing that this is 2018, the stock value has increased by $1,035.93. How does this relate to you? Well, think about what you have spent money on recently or even in 2016. I am sure you blew money on a lot of stuff that you regretted afterward. Monique asked the question that you are probably pondering. "What disposable income did I have?"

Most college kids get this great thing called a refund check from their remaining scholarship, grant, and loan money. If you are not rich, you know all about those refund checks. So, let's just think about this. What would your account look like if you had taken one refund and invested it in Amazon in or before 2016? Let's assume your refund was $3,000 two times a year. What would have happened if you had dedicated $4,800 to Amazon stock and $1,200 for yourself? It is just that simple. It blew me away once I sat down and really thought about the opportunities I've had to be financially independent.

If you grew up like me, you just didn't know any better, so don't beat yourself up. The difference is in the cultures. In the suburban white culture, they are talking about finances on a regular basis. So even if you do have this white kid who gets his hands on an extra $4-6K, he has constantly heard this growing up, so he is more likely to invest his money than a kid from the inner city who has never been taught finances. Now by no means am I telling you that 10K will make you rich but think what happens if you take your profit and reinvest it. I already told you how much money you make off saving your money in a bank, so why do it?

Once I got my first taste of investing, I became addicted to investing my money. If seeing this does not excite you and pique your curiosity, then making money just may not be for you. But if you are a person who loves to run up a bag, then you may want to start doing some research on investing if you haven't already. You don't know what you don't know. So no, I didn't get Amazon for $480, but you can be damn sure I didn't pay $1,515.93 for it either. I hope you found your financial spark before reading this book, but if this book does help, then I will be just as happy. Either way, there is plenty of money to make, so go make you some because it is waiting.

$480 per share x 10 shares = $4,800 total
$1515.93 current price per share - $480 paid price per share = $1,035.93 increase in value per share

$1,515.93 x 10 = $15,159.30 total stock value
$15,159.30 - $4,800 = $10,359.30 profit

"You got to learn the difference between guns and butter. There are two types of niggas, niggas with guns......and niggas with butter. What are the guns? That's the real estate......the stocks and bonds. Artwork. Shit that appreciates with value. What's the butter? Cars, clothes, jewelry, all the bullshit that don't mean shit after you buy it. That's what it's all about: guns and butter."

—Melvin (Ving Rhames), in *Baby Boy* (2001)

CHAPTER 5

Birth of a Business

Starting a business can be hard work, but it can also be very rewarding. The inner cities are filled with businesses that are usually not owned by people in the community. Creating a business for some is the same as creating a child. It goes through some of the same stages: birth, adolescence, maturation, and for some, death. Being a business owner also brings about a sense of pride that can only be matched or surpassed by creating life.

I referenced in chapter 2 the power of the black dollar. As a business owner, you give yourself the opportunity to tap into the black and Hispanic dollar. More important than receiving money, you can create jobs, promote positive change, and assist members of your community. If enough of the community created businesses, they could fix the neighborhood together. In chapter 2 I also referenced how money circulates in the black community. When those businesses start working together, then the money can start circulating around the neighborhood, instead of being given to McDonald's. By the way, McDonald's is not putting it back into your local parks, school programs or even providing something productive for kids to do. I am not saying that you need to be a savior, but you can impact your local community by being an entrepreneur. Aside from that, you may be eligible for certain financial advantages.

There are so many different incentives for being a small business owner. The most beneficial is being awarded tax breaks. What is a tax break? A tax break is a concession or advantage allowed by a government. Why are tax breaks important? Because they can save you some serious money. There are an insane number of tax breaks out there, but I am going to give you only five breaks that are most beneficial to small businesses. At the end of the day, you need to really speak with a tax professional, but I wanted you to know that these things really exist. The benefits of owning a business can really pay dividends, no pun intended.

Opening a business is also a form of investing. Unlike investing, you are very well prepared and did not have to be taught because your creative side comes naturally. What type of business to open is the number one question? Well, the answer is all around you. Look in your community and see what may be lacking or what people are in need of. Happiness is also important, so look at things that interest you. That is what you should open a business in.

Your culture is and has been the hottest thing on the stove for a very long time. This is why so many kids—white, Asian, Latino, and of course, African Americans—listen to the Migos. Suburban whites or valley Asians don't have any idea of what happens in the trap, but you do. From the fashion to the lingo to the latest wave before it goes viral. You usually already know about it. Why? Because you are usually right there in the place of origin. Just listen to your inner voice and trust your creativity. If you do that, then figuring out what business to open won't be as hard as you think—whether you're starting a mobile bar service, designing custom suits for young trendy professionals, or creating an app that randomly picks fingernail polish color. There is a need for all this, so the sky's the limit.

1. **Lunch meetings.** For those of you who love to eat, you may want to consider conducting business over lunch or dinner. If eligible, you can deduct as much as 50 percent of your expense if it is reasonable. That can add up to some serious savings, especially if you eat out every day. Now I don't know of any business that has business lunches every day, but I have seen crazier things happen, so more power to you. Just make sure that you do your homework.

2. **Personal cell phone for business calls.** If a person can clearly distinguish the difference between business and personal calls, then up to 50 percent of your phone bill can be deducted. This can save you half off that $100 phone bill you may have each month. That is approximately $600 per year that can go back in your pocket or toward the business. It would make sense to have an itemized list of calls for proof just in case you are audited, but nevertheless, big savings are possible.

3. **Deduct health care premiums.** Many different factors go into health care, but it is important to know that if you qualify, you may be able to relieve some of that health-care cost.

4. **Manage taxable income.** Let's say you have an LLC (a limited liability company) and are nearing the end of the year. Your business needs to purchase equipment before the end of the fiscal year, and the equipment costs $5,000. Let us assume that your taxable income was 75K. By purchasing the equipment, you may be able to lower your taxable income to 70K, which puts you in a new tax bracket. Hint, hint!

5. **Deduct business travel cost.** If you have business travel-related costs, they can be fully deductible. Airline tickets and rental cars can be really expensive depending on the season. This does not mean you should pretend that you have business in Hawaii every year, but you may want to consider

scheduling a meeting or two around the same time as your vacation. Again, crazier things have happened in this world, so it is possible.

- **Pros to Opening a Business:** *flexibility, pride, potential tax breaks, another source of income*
  While I am not saying that every person in the urban community should open a business, I am saying that doing so can come with some serious upside in the form of financial independence. Have a plan, choose the correct licensing for your business, and do your research to know the correct tax breaks and incentives. Most importantly, choose a product or service that needs consumption. The ultimate goal of every business is to make money.

- **Cons to Opening a Business:** *more responsibility if not the primary source of income, less leisure and personal time, being held personally responsible for others' well-being, a chance to lose everything that was invested*
  Creating a business from the ground up can be very difficult. It requires a lot of research, time, energy, assistance, and usually money. The cons are very similar to investing with one major difference: the law. Depending on the type of business, if you break certain rules, it could not only land you in some financial trouble but also legal trouble. It can go as far as your business being shut down and you being arrested if the regulations are not adhered to. With that type of pressure on the line, you want to make sure that you are paying the proper due diligence to the business.

- **Personal Experience:** My partner and I decided to go into business together, and we figured that an LLC was best for our vision. We decided that we wanted to invest in real estate. It has been a learning experience like no other. Nothing is official yet, but we are in the midst of talks to purchase some commercial real estate as well as some residential real estate before the end of 2018. It is a small step for a large vision, but hey you have to start somewhere. I can tell you that it took some serious research to figure out and decide what line of business I wanted to be in, so we will discuss that.
  People like me think that they can conquer anything. While that may be true, it definitely requires the proper training. So, between real estate, a nightclub, and a gaming lounge for the local community, I was all over the place. I needed to narrow down my choices and focus on one goal at a time. With the help of wise counsel, my business partner, and some of my own thoughts, I decided that real estate, at this point in time, was the most beneficial move for our team. These

are all things to think about. For example, my current career has me on the move a lot, so trying to run a nightclub from another state or even country would not be the smartest decision.

When considering what business to open, be realistic in your approach. If you want to open a restaurant but don't have local family and friends to help you avoid some of the start-up costs, then maybe you need to reconsider. Having your mom run the register or your nephew sweep the floor and your father and his buddies painting the place could all save you big dollars. But not having that type of support means you must do it all yourself, or you will be paying someone else to do it. Again, there are a million things to think about, so just make sure that you are really doing your research, but as discussed earlier, opening a business can absolutely be super rewarding in the end.

"The man I worked for, he had one of the biggest companies in New York City—he ran it for more than fifty years. Fifteen years, eight months, nine days—I was with him every day. I looked after him, took care of him, protected him … I learned from him. Bumpy was rich, but he wasn't white man rich, you see he wasn't wealthy. He didn't own his own company. He thought he did, but he didn't. He just managed it. White man owned it, so they owned him. Nobody owns me, though. Because I own my company. And my company sells a product that's better than the competition at a price that's lower than the competition."

—Frank Lucas (Denzel Washington), in *American Gangster* (2007)

CHAPTER 6

Emergency Funds

Always keep some money tucked away for a rainy day. Growing up in the inner city, I encountered some of the most creative people in the world. "Back in the day," as the old guys used to say, banks were not relied on to keep and protect your money. African Americans specifically did not trust the banks, so they came up with crafty ideas about where to stash their money, no matter their age. The younger guys hid money in shoeboxes, older women stuffed kitchen canisters, and men hid money in the mattress. While technology has evolved, the end results are still the same. You need to store money, valuables, and any other items you deem important. If you still believe in keeping your cash close, then I recommend investing in an actual storage safe.

I understand that funds may be limited, but this is not an investment that should be passed up. Home break-ins happen all the time, so at least you will know that if one does happen, no one is running off with your safe, unless they are the Incredible Hulk! The part of debt that is not talked about enough is emergency debt. Usually you will hear about student debt, automotive debt, home loans, and credit card debt, but there is one more that causes issues. The truth is that emergencies happen more often than one would believe, and they usually are very costly once they do happen. The emergency comes in many different forms—car repairs, medical co-pays, or a leaky pipe that needs to be replaced. These things can cause a major financial burden. How can one be prepared for these unexpected situations?

I am sure that you all have heard of the money challenge chart. If you have not, then it is a chart that encourages a person to save predetermined amounts of money daily, weekly, or even monthly. This can be altered to fit anyone's specific needs, and capabilities, so find out what circumstances benefit you. I found that the challenge worked best for me when I did it weekly. My first challenge started January 1, 2016. My chart increased by $2 per week. By the end of the fifty-two weeks, I had saved $2,756.00. While this may seem like a lot, it worked for me at the time. Remember, the key is to pick an increase that is compatible with your financial situation. There are numerous savings charts available with different amounts that you can choose from and make it personal.

Week	Deposit Amount	Account Balance	Week	Deposit Amount	Account Balance
1	$2.00	$2.00	27	$54.00	$756.00
2	$4.00	$6.00	28	$56.00	812.00
3	$6.00	$12.00	29	$58.00	$870.00
4	$8.00	$20.00	30	$60.00	$930.00
5	$10.00	$30.00	31	$62.00	$992.00
6	$12.00	$42.00	32	$64.00	$1,056.00
7	$14.00	$56.00	33	$66.00	$1,122.00
8	$16.00	$72.00	34	$68.00	$1,190.00
9	$18.00	$90.00	35	$70.00	$1,260.00
10	$20.00	$110.00	36	$72.00	$1,332.00
11	$22.00	$132.00	37	$74.00	$1,406.00
12	$24.00	$156.00	38	$76.00	$1,482.00
13	$26.00	$182.00	39	$78.00	$1,560.00
14	$28.00	$210.00	40	$80.00	$1,640.00
15	$30.00	$240.00	41	$82.00	$1,722.00
16	$32.00	$272.00	42	$84.00	$1,806.00
17	$34.00	$306.00	43	$86.00	$1,892.00
18	$36.00	$342.00	44	$88.00	$1,980.00
19	$38.00	$380.00	45	$90.00	$2,070.00
20	$40.00	$420.00	46	$92.00	$2,162.00
21	$42.00	$462.00	47	$94.00	$2,256.00
22	$44.00	$506.00	48	$96.00	$2,352.00
23	$46.00	$552.00	49	$98.00	$2,450.00
24	$48.00	$600.00	50	$100.00	$2,550.00
25	$50.00	$650.00	51	$102.00	$2,652.00
26	$52.00	$702.00	52	$104.00	$2,756.00

The challenge is more than just saving money; it teaches you discipline and patience and also gives you self-confidence in your ability to save. For all the hypercompetitive people out there, you can make a game out of this challenge. I was able to rationalize this challenge as a game in my mind, which added a fun twist to it. I mean, who doesn't love a good game every now and then? The easiest parts of this challenge are the first few weeks, but believe you me, it does get difficult. Unfortunately, I couldn't complete my goal of fifty-two consecutive weeks of saving with no errors. Once you start missing weeks, it can become a snowball effect. If this happens, in order to maintain the challenge, you must then double up on weeks. If you miss week one, then week two will require two deposits. After you reach week twenty-five on the chart, playing catch-up could be extremely difficult, so avoid missing deposits if at all possible.

The first four weeks won't mean as much because you may have a $20 bill lying around here or there. Beyond that, it starts taking some serious dedication for the remainder of the chart. This is when the weekly amount may no longer be readily available and may require an ATM run. The solution to this may be a biweekly deposit since most Americans get paid biweekly, on the first and the fifteenth.

Let's break down how this goal can be completed over a fifty-two-week period. The week 52 deposit is $104.00 per the chart ($104.00/7 days = 14.86), approximately $15.00 per day. The United States military calls this process "backward planning." To some people this may be a lot of money every day for food, and those are probably the people who take their lunch to work. For my readers who love Starbucks or do not cook as often, $15.00 per day may be normal. Let's say for my non-cookers that we went one week without buying Starbucks coffee and lunch. The total weekly savings could be as much as our week fifty-two savings. I understand this may be hard for some, so be reasonable in your abilities. I am not saying to go fifty-two weeks without a coffee, but I am saying to limit yourself if this will potentially help you save $104.00 per week.

- **Pros of Establishing an Emergency Fund:** *cash on hand and available, learning how to save, avoiding debt due to lack of emergency funds, building financial confidence*
I know that some people believe that credit cards are a form of emergency relief, and in some cases that may be true. Keep in mind that your credit card is not interest free, which means you are paying additional money to the card company. The payment may be delayed, which allows you to believe that you dodged a bullet when in reality, you just paid more over a longer period of time. Keep something tucked away for a rainy day and make that your emergency money if ever something comes up. I am not saying keep 10K cash on hand but keep an amount that is suitable for your needs and income. For major life emergencies you can use the credit card, but for a few hundred or maybe even a couple thousand, your emergency stash could cover that.

- **Cons of Establishing an Emergency Fund:** *another weekly task to account for, unnecessary trips to the ATM, large amounts of money stored in your home*
Hiding money in the house may be extra work, but for those of you who know a friend of a friend who does shady stuff, this could be beneficial. Hey, by no means am I saying go buy stolen property, but when that sixty-five-inch curved Samsung falls off the truck by accident for $700 when the retail price is $1,499 and you know that you wanted a television, you're going to wish that you had that emergency money on hand!

• **Personal Experience:** My emergency fund did not come out of necessity but desire. Prior to starting my fifty-two-week challenge at the start of 2016, I had missed out on a great deal, which is what sparked the idea of having real emergency money on hand.

I am a serious cologne collector. I love to smell good, and while I have a great collection, I do not have any Bond No. 9. Now if you know anything about this stuff, it smells amazing, like head-turning amazing. When I was an intern at a premier high-end retailer, I would pitch this to my male customers, and if they were with their wives, the women would always shut the sale down. The response was usually, "I don't want him smelling this good unless he's with me." The guys would get a kick out of seeing their wives jealous. I must admit, it was cute. The price of Bond ranges from $230.00 to $350.00. I hoped that I would find a substitute so I would not have to pay that amount for it, but I still have not. Nevertheless, I was at home when I got a call from my brother, telling me there was a guy at the barbershop selling cologne. I usually would not have cared or even gone out of my way, but he told me that this guy had some Bond. I asked for a picture, and to my surprise, this dude actually had the eau de parfum! The gentleman selling the cologne had it in its original package and everything. He was asking $250 for one bottle. I spoke with him on the phone and assured him that I would purchase two bottles today if I could get them for $400 total. He told me that he was not holding any merchandise, but that if he had them when I got there, we had a deal. This was a time when having some cash on hand would have come in handy. Unfortunately, there was not an ATM close to where I was staying, and this guy only wanted cash. I was definitely breaking the speed limit trying to find a bank teller. I finally made it, got the money, and proceeded to the barbershop. By the time I got there, the guy had sold all the merchandise and was walking out the door. I was pissed! I took his number in hopes that he would come across some more Bond, but it's now 2018, and I still don't have any Bond. I do plan on investing in my first bottle this year. If I had some emergency cash on hand, then I could have purchased both bottles and saved myself roughly $300, not including tax.

Now while this was not a true emergency, the same could apply for emergencies. The truth is, you aren't just saving for an emergency; you're saving for the right opportunity. You just never know, so it is better to be safe rather than sorry. By the way, revisiting the feeling of missing out on my Bond has been difficult, very difficult.

"Shout out to the homeowners, the girls that got diplomas and enough money to loan us, a little something extra should we ever need it. If it sounds like you then let me hear you repeat it."

—Drake (Aubrey Graham), *Thank Me Later* (2010)

CHAPTER 7

Map Your Spending

The most frequently asked question when it comes to planned spending is, "Where do I start?" The first step needs to be identifying what is necessary to you. The most dangerous part of spending money is not necessarily the amount but the rush that comes from the perceived benefit. Not having a specific plan or list of exact needs causes people to unnecessarily spend every time. The technical term for this by retailers is "impulse buying."

There are multiple ways to avoid impulsive shopping. One of the best ways of fixing a problem is to separate yourself from the source of the problem. By leaving your debit card at home, you are doing exactly that—tremendously cutting down your chances of overspending by excessive swiping. Not to mention saving yourself the chance of your banking information leaking into the wrong hands. I'm not saying that these retail stores aren't taking the necessary steps to protect your identity, but it is just that—*your* identity. No one will protect you like you.

Cyberattacks are on the rise, not just with retail stores; cyberhackers even went as far as meddling in the 2016 presidential election. This is just food for thought. The less you can give someone regarding your personal information, the better. I get that cryptocurrency is the new wave, but for the time being, cash is still here.

If you substitute cash for your card, a few things can happen. You may be able to budget more effectively as well as maintain balances in real time. I know what you are thinking—isn't that the purpose of banking apps? While banking apps tell you your balance, without constant monitoring, your charges can get out of hand quickly. Looking in your pocket is a much quicker solution.

Think of your debit card as a weapon. Now think about your finances as the ammunition. If not used in moderation, this ammunition can render the weapon useless. Every time you swipe that card, it is like shooting a gun. Unless you are a weapons expert who knows the exact weight and feel of a gun after each round has been fired, then there is no way possible for you to know how many bullets remain in the weapon. This is equivalent to using your debit card all "willy-nilly", as my grandma used to say. Just like the solution to your gun problem is keeping count of each bullet fired or shooting until it is empty, so is the process for your daily finances. Either of these methods would work, though I am seriously against the latter of the two.

Experienced gun owners do not carelessly fire a weapon for several different reasons. The most important thing is that with no predetermined target, the round can go anywhere. The same holds true for your finances. This means your cash also needs a daily target. Using cash is not only how you budget, but it is also how you save money. By giving yourself a daily or weekly allowance, you can cut out a lot of bad spending habits. This method will keep you honest. If you are shopping in the store and spot a pair of jeans that costs $40.00, but you only have $50.00 for the week and you have yet to put gas in your car, then I am almost sure of your decision. The smarter person would choose to put gas in their vehicle.

I am certain that I am not the only person who knows individuals who like to live life on the edge. Those folks may just decide to roll the dice, thinking that gas is not a necessary daily function, and purchase the jeans. The purpose of having cash on hand is to autocorrect your impulsive buying habit by limiting your ability to purchase. On the other hand, if you are one of those people who like to push the envelope and live life on the edge, then by all means, purchase the jeans.

A $50 budget may or may not be enough for you to shop comfortably. That is part of the benefits of having cash on hand. You can budget and successfully track how much money you spend because you know how much you start with each day. You also know exactly where your money went because that will probably be your only purchase for the week, other than necessities. I don't know of anyone who checks their account every single day unless they are specifically waiting for something to hit the account. I can promise you it isn't that hard to remember where your $50.00 went when $40.00 of it was applied toward a pair of jeans.

- **Pros to Mapping Your Spending:** *reduce impulse buying, limit identity theft, save money*
Having a plan for your spending makes life so much easier. You really get a chance to see gains, build that financial confidence, and even pinpoint possible bad spending habits. When you have a lot more disposable income, this is not that big of a deal. But when you have a child, are looking to buy a home, or even saving for that dream vacation, identifying where your money is going is pivotal for the saving process. If you can get it now, then you will seriously be ahead of the curve and on easy street when it comes to obtaining your goals.

- **Cons to Mapping Your Spending:** *more frequent ATM trips, cash to account for*
I will admit, driving to the ATM every single week at times felt stupid and like a waste of time. Stick with it, and if you are consistent, the benefits will show up in more ways than one. Once you get past that initial surge, then those feelings of stupidity will turn into a sense of accomplishment. I'll drop this on your plate. Companies pay people serious dollars to do for them what you are doing for yourself. Those people are called auditors, accountants, and financial managers. You,

my friend, are the total package. While you may not have the fancy certifications and licenses to go along with it, you can master the art of a fat account.

- **Personal Experience:** I wrote a financial plan. The plan was pretty detailed, but I also have experience doing this, so for beginners, just try to capture a week's worth of transactions. After you've gotten your week in the book, then multiply that by four to get your total for the month. This, of course, is only if you are a beginner. If you are a seasoned planner, then lay out your detailed plan in order to track your purchases, but you don't have to make your financial plan super fancy. An example of a simple financial plan is food, gas, and leisure. These are daily essentials that should not take much for you to figure out.

   After you have the plan, take your money out of the bank at whatever frequency fits your lifestyle. That may be weekly or biweekly. Either way, that is a part of the plan. My plan consisted of a weekly withdrawal. The weekly withdrawal worked for me because I was eliminating debit card use, budgeting, and doing the fifty-two-week challenge. Yes, I know what you're thinking—it is a lot and I agree it was challenging, but it was fun pushing myself to try to manage all three at one time. I recommend trying one at a time because together they can really be a headache.

"Whatever your financial goal is, whether it's buying a house, traveling or investing, what is one simple task you can take today, quickly? So many people look at the task as a whole, but goals are merely a collection of small tasks put together. Just do something every day, simple and soon."

—Tiffany "The Budgetnista" Aliche

CHAPTER 8

Understanding Demand & Supply

To understand demand and supply, you must understand retail. To understand retail, you must first get into the mind of consumers. Retailers oftentimes don't get enough credit for how good they are at understanding their target market. They pump serious money into understanding their customers and the customers' desires. We often feel like we have to have the newest and latest things to come out. This includes anything from cars, homes, and cellular phones, to baby products. Our desire to have new, most of the time, does not have anything to do with innovation versus how we have been programmed. The internet has really made the world smaller. In real time we can see new products released. Oftentimes we purchase those things because our idols, role models, or the person we follow on IG has them. We do this, not understanding that the item was just released and will be extremely expensive due to its visibility. Unless you stay under a rock, then you know that purchasing during the hype comes with a hefty price tag. Wait on purchasing new and let the market calm down. Once the initial surge has subsided, you may find a better deal.

Yes, I am very aware of the title of this section and how unorthodox it is. I am a believer in what Andre Coleman from *Power* said, which is referenced below in the quote for this chapter. Nothing in the world has truly ever been created, only recreated. Every idea and thought is derived from a previous idea or thought. We use the universe to draw inspiration and develop things out of necessity or desire. Both feelings are directly intertwined with demand. I don't see supply as the beginning, even though every credible marketing and business school in the United States teaches supply and demand. The first rule of being an entrepreneur is to recognize a problem. This is Small Business 101; you are a problem solver who owns a business, not a business owner who solves problems.

To put this into context for my orthodox readers, I will explain it as it has normally been taught. The law of supply states that the quantity of goods supplied rises as the market price rises and falls as the price falls. Let's take, for example, hoverboards. The boards made their debut in 2015 and were the hottest Christmas item of the year. The prices of the hoverboard ranged from $300.00 unbranded to $1,800 for the branded ones. Celebrities from Wiz Khalifa to J. R. Smith made appearances on the hoverboard. "By the end of 2015, 40,000 boards were coming into the United States each day" (Cendrowski). While total sales were not tracked, manufacturers have shipped more than $2 billion worth of hoverboards over the past year and a half. Over the past year, hoverboards have been dying off. The nail in the coffin was the national announcement that deemed the boards unsafe.

As always when you have a successful item, you have people trying to mimic that success. The boards started malfunctioning when competition started creating knockoff boards with cheaper materials. Sales immediately declined worldwide, and most companies have gone out of business. The number of boards produced per day was extremely high while the market price was high. Now that the price is low, you won't see nearly as many hoverboards in stock. If someone does have a large quantity, it is probably because they are getting them at a deeply discounted rate.

Now the law of demand states that the quantity of a good demanded falls as the price rises, and as the price falls, demand rises. Let's use televisions as our example of how demand works. The demand for larger televisions has increased for the past ten years. It is hard to pinpoint what exactly made the demand increase. Experts could argue innovation, economics, or even advertising. I personally believe it is a mixture of all those reasons. However, I do believe Black Friday, which is the single most profitable day for American retailers, plays a huge part in this equation. With almost every retailer now participating in the American holiday, business is good. According to the *Washington Post*, "There has been a 10 percent year-to-date increase in the number of TV's sold that are larger than 50 inches." Following the law of demand, this was possible because of the drop-in price. In the same article, the *Washington Post* goes on to say, "While prices for televisions are down 5 percent year-over-year, they're down nearly 19 percent for sets that are 65 to 69 inches." So how does this all connect? The demand for larger televisions increased when the price of those products decreased.

If it still doesn't make sense to you, I will break it down. TVs in general have been on the decline lately. This could be for a number of reasons, specifically the popularity of Black Friday over the past decade. This probably means that people were consuming more televisions per household, since this was retailers' ticketed item. Either way, when the price of oversize TVs started going down, then people started buying more. Understanding consumers can get very tricky, but the market is the market, and usually this holds true no matter the scenario. So, for all you people who purchase things as soon as they are released, hopefully this helps you think next time. Stop being in such a rush and let the market show its hand. If the product is good enough, then they will make an updated version, and you can get the now older version for cheaper. So, the next time you want to purchase something pricey, think about demand and supply. Companies understand that their business is a copycat league. They want to drop a product and make as much money as they can before the competition figures out what is happening and releases a similar product. When multiple companies release an almost identical product, a few things are happening.

1. *The other companies have monitored the market and believe the new wave is profitable.*
2. *They do not want to allow their competitors to have unchallenged market share.*

3. A company believes that they can make the product at a cheaper price. Once this happens, they usually flood the market and bully other companies' sales away.

This is usually a very good sign for you, the consumer. Barring certain staple items with little to no competition, most items decline in price when multiple companies release a similar item. This is due to something called market saturation. Companies know when consumers have too many options, they can quickly lose interest in buying from a specific company. With competition the price is now the determining factor. They know once the market is saturated, then it is time to drop the price. Once one company starts this drop, it is a downward spiral that requires all the others to drop their prices. This is when you really start winning as a consumer. When you understand demand and supply or supply and demand, you can wait for the appropriate time and take advantage of the market.

- **Pros to Understanding Demand and Supply:** *market identification, knowing when to and when not to buy investments, saving money*

  In class, once we got down to the science behind why people consume what they consume, it became fascinating to say the least. I wouldn't worry so much about the how and why because that requires a little more knowledge of the system. If I were you, I would focus on demand and supply. You could dodge some major bullets and save some serious coin at the same time.

- **Cons to Understanding Demand and Supply:** *being potentially the last person in your social circle to have a new item, requires research of the product and a following of the market*

  Does it really matter that the girls in your circle had their bloody shoes before you, if you got two pairs for the price of their one? Nobody cares how long you had something if you have it. So just keep that in mind. For my male readers, it won't matter if two years ago, you were staying with your mom to save money. When your lady friend comes to visit your new condo overlooking uptown Charlotte, it won't matter where you were two years ago. You had a plan, you executed that plan, and you stayed disciplined. Now you look like the person who really has their financial situation figured out.

- **Personal Experience:** A few chapters back I mentioned having a Cole Haan fetish, well here it is. I own seven pairs of Cole Haans, and four of them are the exact same style—they're just different colors. I guess that speaks to my love for the shoe. They have been around for a while, but a few years ago, the company decided to end their partnership with Nike. To somebody else it may have meant they were just ending their partnership, but to me this meant that my favorite shoe would be going on sale soon to make room for their new line excluding the Nike technology.

I waited for about nine months, and finally the price started to drop. Once the company released a newer version of the shoe post-Nike, then the previous model was dropped.

Now I know what you may be thinking: "It's just a shoe." Well, my friend, the Cole Haan Lunargrand can cost you anywhere from $220 to $265. So I waited until my time came, and then I went and purchased four at one time. To some it might be crazy, but between knowing the price drop was coming and saving for the day, I was all set to purchase the pair I had been eyeballing. This purchase incorporated a few aspects of financial discipline, like saving, having emergency money, and mapping my spending. While this was not anything major like a sixty-five-inch, curved, smart TV, it was something that I really wanted. You too can do the same for whatever it is that you want, but you must be patient and prepared.

"Demand and supply, they've been teaching that wrong for years. Demand comes first, and whoever supplies it profits."

—Andre Coleman (Olurotimi Akinosho) in *Power* (2015)

CHAPTER 9

Travel

It may sound like an oxymoron, seeing that you are reading a book about saving money, yet the title of this chapter is travel. Traveling requires spending one of the very things attempting to be saved. In all actuality, though, there is just as much benefit to traveling as there is to saving money. I have identified three major benefits.

The first of the three is the human element. Before the internet arrived, people shared information mostly in person. Though the World Wide Web has diminished this process, it can never truly be done away with. There are things that can only be learned by being present for the lesson. Personal face time with a person who has a different set of experiences is priceless. There are no accurate data found to express how many ideas come from human versus nonhuman interactions, but I am almost positive the number tremendously favors human interactions. Very few things in life are created; most are just reinvented. The famous inventor Lewis Latimer said it best: "Some blessings have been ours in the past, and these may be repeated or even multiplied."

The second benefit of travel, but the most important to me, is that everyone loves a vacation. The correlation between happiness and good health has been proven. The people who are truly the happiest in life are most likely the healthiest. Traveling is a method to relieve stress. On average, American employees receive twelve to fourteen days' vacation time per year. Great Britain averages twenty-six, and France has a minimum of thirty days per year. The United States was fourteenth out of 155 countries on the happy index for the years 2014 to 2016. The United States has since fallen four spots and is now eighteenth out of 155 countries. Finland topped the list this year, moving up four spots. The Finns average approximately twenty-five days of annual vacation time for their employees. While you may not be able to dictate the number of vacation days you receive from your employer, you can still set up an annual trip. This may assist you in your pursuit of a clear mind and contribute to a happy spirit and a healthy body.

Travel

Shown below for your reference is the latest World Happiness Report.

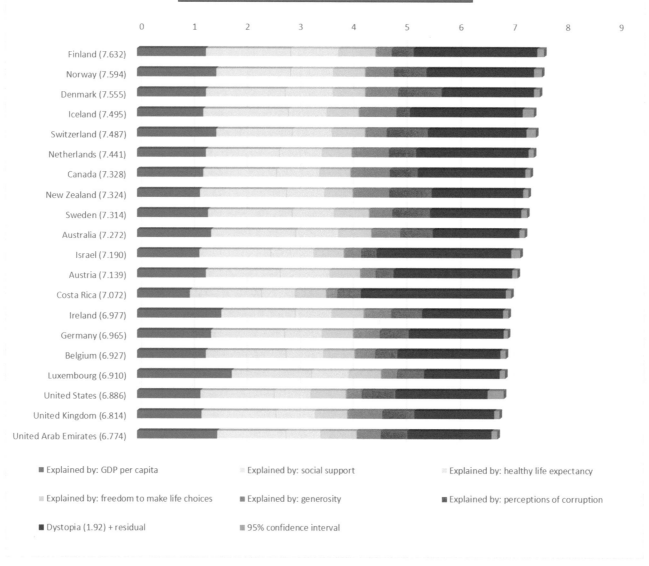

48

The third and final benefit to traveling that I want to mention is becoming educated on different cultures. This exposure to a different set of beliefs, norms, and customs should expand your horizons. Just because you are good at something does not mean there isn't a better way to do it. When I was growing up, my mother would tell me all the time, "If you want to know what not to do, watch and listen to a dummy." Knowing what not to do is just as important as knowing what to do. Now by no means am I saying that people from other places are dummies, and Americans have it all figured out. Obviously, we are not even close as a country to having things figured out. If you can somehow figure out what not to do with your money, then there is no limit on what you can accomplish with the money you do have.

- **Pros to Traveling:** *gain cultural enlightenment, relieve stress, expand mental capacity, have fun and make new friends*
  Traveling can and will change your life. The funny thing about it is this will happen immediately! You don't have to wait on this to kick in. As soon as you experience someone else's culture, it immediately does something to you. Even greater than experiencing someone else's culture is that when you get a chance to experience your own cultural background and ancestry firsthand, it changes your entire trajectory.

- **Cons to Traveling:** *spending money*
  Money will come and money will go, but the benefit that you get from traveling far outweighs the negatives. If you have ever traveled, then you should be able to relate to this. If you have not, then it will make more sense once you do.

- **Personal Experience:** Traveling away from America changed my life. I personally have been able to expand my horizons and become more culturally educated and financially literate through my travels. Even though I have been fortunate enough to have traveled, there is still so much more for me to see and learn. Currently my country count is at twenty. I cannot honestly tell you that traveling is the only reason for this growth because that just wouldn't be the truth. Travel, maturation, and education are all a part of my growth. What I can say is that my personal exposure to other people, places, ideas, and beliefs has been the most influential thing to happen to me.
  I hope you have all seen the movie *Black Panther*. For those of my readers who have not, you should. *"Wakanda Forever"*! One friend who knows that I have been to Africa twice called me and asked if it was really like that. I told him the movie did the best they could, but no movie can even come close to what you feel when you are there. Everything about the continent is

astonishing. Africa has a special place in my heart because this is where my ancestors are from. This is where life was created. Furthermore, before going, I never had a chance to experience the culture, people, or places. So again, travel, explore, and open your mind, heart, and soul to other people, places, and things.

"To travel is to expand … to expand is to grow … to grow is to change … and to change is your destiny. Everything that has life goes on a journey—why should you be excluded?"

—Christopher Lawson

MY INSPIRATION

My inspiration for this book came from a few different encounters or lack thereof. First, I don't see enough African Americans in the financial world. I am not sure if that is due to fear or tradition. We can always use more African American CFOs and CEOs. My reason for writing this book was because it was my way of giving back to the community. However, this book is not just for African Americans but anyone from the inner city who has had, is having, or will have financial struggles. If I can in any way prevent or help prevent that from happening by providing any knowledge that I have accumulated over my short lifetime, then I feel that it is my duty to give back. I never had anyone come to my high school and talk to me about finances in a way that was relatable. I didn't need all the answers, just an introduction in my language. Which in my opinion is just as important as, if not more important than, the lesson itself.

Hopefully this book connects a few dots or sparks a thought that otherwise would not have been thought about. Other communities have this conversation all the time, which is one of the reasons why they are more financially sound. It is time that we start doing the same as a community. Money makes the world go around, so we should understand how to use, save, manipulate, and take complete advantage of this commodity.

I hope this book helps anyone who reads it because you were my inspiration, so thank you.

Sincerely,

Christopher Lawson

Endnotes

Chapter 1
Short, Doug. October 14, 2016. "Median Household Income by State: A New Look at the Data." https://www.advisorperspectives.com/dshort/updates/2016/10/14/median-household-income-by-state-a-new-look-at-the-data.

Chapter 2
Noël, Reginald A. November 5, 2014. "Income and Spending Patterns among Black Households." https://www.bls.gov/opub/btn/volume-3/income-and-spending-patterns-among-black-households.htm.
Brian. 2015. "Black Buying Power to Reach $1.3 Trillion by 2017." http://www.blackentrepreneur.com/black-buying-power-to-reach-1-3-trillion-by-2017/.
Nielsen. September 19, 2013. "African-American Consumers Are More Relevant than Ever." http://www.nielsen.com/us/en/insights/news/2013/african-american-consumers-are-more-relevant-than-ever.html.

Thaii. July 26, 2017). "Asians Keep a Dollar in Their Community 120 Times Longer than African Americans." https://www.themaven.net/blackwealthchannel/community-building/asians-keep-a-dollar-in-their-community-120-times-longer-than-african-americans-2ZvNTGNxpkClloXlXK_wMQ.
Helm Bronner, Angela. June 5, 2016. "Black Women Now the Most Educated Group in U.S." https://www.theroot.com/black-women-now-the-most-educated-group-in-us-1790855540.

Chapter 3
Mayer, Brittany. March 15, 2017. "300–850: The Credit Score Range Explained (FICO & VantageScore)." https://www.badcredit.org/how-to/credit-score-range/.
Merriam-Webster. 1828. Definition of Leverage. https://www.merriam-webster.com/dictionary/leverage.

Chapter 4
Nielsen. March 5, 2015. "Smartphone Owners Are As Diverse As Their Devices." http://www.nielsen.com/us/en/insights/news/2015/smartphone-owners-are-as-diverse-as-their-devices.html.
Value Penguin. 2018. "Average Savings Account Interest Rates for 2018: Compared across Banks." https://www.valuepenguin.com/average-savings-account-interest-rates.

Navy Federal Credit Union. 2017. Easy Start Investor by Navy Federal Financial Group." https://www.easystartinvestor.com/easystart/home.

Chapter 5
English Oxford Living Dictionaries. Definition of Tax Break. https://en.oxforddictionaries.com/definition/tax_break.

Chapter 6
Coordinated Kate. January 2, 2014. "Financial Tip Friday! 52 Week Money Challenge Revised." https://coordinatedkate.com/2014/01/02/financial-tip-thursday-52-week-money-challenge-revised/.

Chapter 7

Chapter 8
Cendrowski, Scott. March 4, 2016. "Boom Goes the Hoverboard Fad." http://fortune.com/hoverboard-industry/. Halzack, Sarah. November 24, 2015. "The Rise of the Really-Big-Screen TV." https://www.washingtonpost.com/news/business/wp/2015/11/24/the-rise-of-the-really-big-screen-tv/?utm_term=.eb53ec6a9d21.

Chapter 9
World Happiness Report. March 14, 2018. "World Happiness Report." http://www.dayofhappiness.net/report/. Gadd, Michael. August 21, 2014. "Americans Get the Least Paid Vacation Time in the World—While Others Countries Enjoy As Many As Forty Days Off a Year." http://www.dailymail.co.uk/news/article-2730947/Americans-paid-vacation-time-world-countries-enjoy-FORTY-days-year.html.

About the Author

I am just a guy from the inner city of Columbia, South Carolina. A guy who was able to use his environment as fuel and his mistakes as lessons. I have always been intrigued with money. My passion for money, along with my ability to sprint, eventually took me to college. I graduated from the University of South Carolina with a bachelor's degree in Retail Management. It was here where I was able to challenge my educational boundaries.

Upon graduation, I interned with Nordstrom, where I learned a lot about the inner workings of the retail industry. Soon after, I went on to receive an additional degree in Financial Management when I joined the Air Force as a Financial Comptroller. At times as a young Airman, I oversaw multimillion-dollar budgets very early in my career. This experience was paramount in my quest for financial enlightenment.

I was fortunate enough to learn a great deal about government budgeting, management, and spending. Along with having financial exposure, I was also able to rack up some serious air miles in my three years with the Air Force, I visited over twenty countries on humanitarian missions. These missions included everything from currency exchange and fee negotiation to multi pallet drop-offs. I have since gone on to pursue other endeavors in both my military and civilian careers. The book on Christopher Lawson is still being written, so stay tuned.

Printed in the United States
By Bookmasters